Holy Gnostic Liturgy

of the

Pleromic Light

We are pleased to present this Personal Missal edition of our principal liturgy which may be used by clergy and congregation alike. This edition is identical to that found in the ACP Clergy Handbook and the ACP Lectionary for Mass. It is our hope and prayer that this small work will enrich the experience of all participants.

HOLY GNOSTIC LITURGY

OF THE

PLEROMIC LIGHT

TriadPress

Fox Lake, IL

The Holy Gnostic Liturgy of the Pleromic Light

Personal Missal Edition
Published 2025

ISBN-13: 978-0-9973101-3-9

Triad Press, LLC
123 S. US 12 #33
Fox Lake, IL 60020

Scan for a list of titles available from Triad Press

The Holy Gnostic Liturgy of the Pleromic Light

Introductory Note

The Holy Gnostic Liturgy of the Pleromic Light is the central rite of the Apostolic Church of the Pleroma. While the principal celebrant of the Mass is the priest or bishop, there are crucial roles for every level of clergy. It will benefit you greatly to learn not only your own unique role, but to study and become intimately familiar with every aspect of the liturgy. The Holy Mass has many truths to impart, and many mysteries to reveal to the one who carefully studies, contemplates, and meditates upon its many-faceted teachings. The better acquainted you are with the liturgy, the more you will get out of each celebration of the Most Holy Eucharist, and the better prepared you will be to fulfill your own ecclesiastical duties. Within the Liturgy of the Pleromic Light, you will find expressed the highest of Hermetic and Qabalistic principles, as well as the most sublime formulas of alchemical and theurgic operations. Just as Christ is the great Mediator, so too is His Holy Sacrament the means by which all doctrines are reconciled, and the soul itself may experience regeneration and reintegration into the fullness of God.

Temple Layout

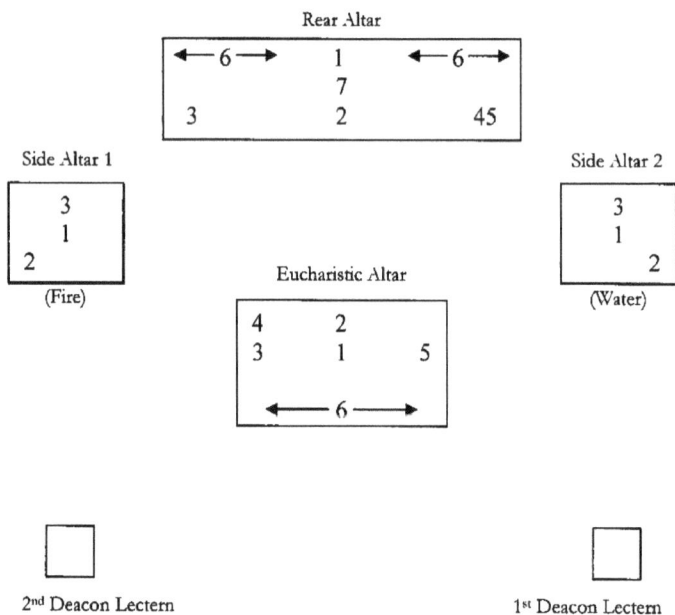

Rear Altar

← 6 →	1	← 6 →
	7	
3	2	45

Side Altar 1

	3
	1
2	

(Fire)

Side Altar 2

3	
1	
	2

(Water)

Eucharistic Altar

4	2	
3	1	5
← 6 →		

2nd Deacon Lectern

1st Deacon Lectern

P

E

L

A

— — — — — —
— — —C∴C∴— — ·
— — — — — —

— — — — — —
— — —C∴C∴— — ·
— — — — — —

Temple Layout Key

Rear Altar

1. Seven-stick candelabra
2. Lectionary
3. Thurible
4. **Aspergillum**
5. Lavabo font
6. Icons
7. Sword (pointing North)

Eucharistic Altar

1. **Altar stone, Chalice, etc.**
2. Scripture (open to Gosp. Jn.)
3. Ceremonial Dagger
4. **Bell**
5. Ciborium
6. Altar Cross & Icons

Side Altar 1

1. **Perpetual Luminary**
2. Other special or occasional items
3. Icons

Side Altar 2

1. Wine & Water cruets
2. Other special or occasional items
3. Icons

P = Porters
L = Lectors
E = Exorcists
A = Acolytes

C ∴ C ∴ = Congregants

Preliminary Rites

Before each celebration of the Holy Liturgy, the participating clergy shall assemble in the antechamber for certain preliminary rites, prayers, and meditation. Before vesting, each of the clergy should make the following prayer over his or her vestments:

"Our help is in the Name of the Lord. Bless these cloths, and make for me a robe of your Incorruptible Light. Amen."

Next, an Acolyte should enter the Temple proper and light the Perpetual Luminary. When the Acolyte returns, the Thurifer - who should be an Exorcist - proceeds to cense the Temple as he or she has been previously instructed. The Thurifer then returns to the antechamber with the thurible and prepares for procession. The Porter then calls the clergy to order thus:

"My Brothers and Sisters, come to order and prepare yourselves for our procession into the Temple of the Most High God."

The clergy will then line up in the following order:

• Porters (principal Porter acting as Conductor and carrying Sword)
• Lectors (principal Lector carrying Gospel)
• Exorcists (principal Exorcist carrying Altar Cross)
• Acolytes (principal Acolyte carrying Eucharistic elements)
• Deacons
• Priests
• Bishops

- Visiting Bishops
- Eparchs
- Exarch
- Patriarch
- Thurifer (should be of the rank of Exorcist)

Once the clergy has lined up for procession, they shall place their right hand over the heart while the Lector offers the following Invocation of the Paraclete:

"O Mother-Father of the Aeons,
O Paraclete!
Spirit of Truth,
Omnipresent and filling everything, Giver of Life!
Come to dwell in us,
Purify us of all iniquities
And save our souls,
O Merciful God!"

Then all clergy together say:

"Through our Lord Jesus, Christos, Soter, Logos. Amen."

The officiating Priest then calls for a moment of silent meditation and reflection. After a couple of minutes, the Porter says:

"My Brothers and Sisters, let us now enter the Temple of the Most High with the reverence due the Sovereign Architect of All Worlds."

Procession

The clergy processes single file into the Temple, circum-ambulating the Eucharistic Altar three times clockwise. On the first circuit, the Holy Bible is placed on the Altar open to the Gospel According to John. On the second circuit, the Altar Cross is placed in position. On the third circuit, the Eucharistic elements are placed on their appropriate altars. After the third circuit, the clergy lines up a few feet in front of the Eucharistic Altar. However, the Porter bearing the Sword remains standing centered behind the clergy line, and the Exorcist who is acting as Thurifer stands directly behind the Porter, continuing to swing the thurible from side to side while the opening invocations are recited.

Invocation of the Aeons

PRIEST:
In the Name of the Lord of all Worlds.

Priest and Deacons place right hand over heart.

PRIEST:
I...

1ˢᵗ DEACON:
A...

2ⁿᵈ DEACON:
O...

Priest and Deacons place hands, right over left, over the Solar Plexus.

PRIEST:
I…

1ˢᵗ DEACON:
A…

2ⁿᵈ DEACON
UM…

> *Priest & Deacons cross their arms across chest, right over left, palms open.*

PRIEST:
A…

1ˢᵗ DEACON:
U…

2ⁿᵈ DEACON:
M…

> *Clergy now place their hands in front of them, palms together, as in prayer.*

PRIEST:
Lord of the Past

PRIEST & DEACONS: *(As all take one step forward)*
We hail thee!

PRIEST:
Lord of the Present

PRIEST & DEACONS: *(As all take one step forward)*
We hail thee!

PRIEST:
Lord of the Future

PRIEST & DEACONS *(As all take one step forward)*
We hail thee!

CLERGY: *(Kneeling before the Eucharistic Altar)*
O Ineffable Light, Father of Resplendent Glory, Mother of
Eternal Wisdom, we, being assembled together on the path of
Light to manifest the Power of the Logos, the Christ within,
and to participate in the offering of that great sacrifice which
was, and is, and is to come, do hail Thee as the Great Architect
of the Universe, and the Source of all Light, Life, Love, and
Liberty.

Clergy rise and proceed to their stations. Porter places Sword
on Rear Altar, pointing North, and proceeds to station at the
Temple entrance. Thurifer replaces thurible on Rear Altar and
proceeds to station.

PRIEST:
In the Name of the Unknown One who reveals His Mysteries
out of the Treasuries of Light to them that call upon Him, and
who mercifully bestows His Secrets of Gnosis upon us without
measure.

May He always grant to us, through Christ the Eternal Logos, and the Divine Sophia, the revealer of His Gnosis, His eternal blessings that we may worthily perform the mysteries of the Mass. Help us to reveal the greatest Secrets which are lawful for man to know, and use them without offence unto God. Amen.

PRIEST:
For what purpose do we congregate?

1st DEACON:
To seek Truth.

PRIEST:
What shall we use to aid us in our search for Truth?

2nd DEACON: *(using a small taper, extracts flame from Perpetual Luminary)*
The Light of Gnosis!

PRIEST: *(receives lit taper from Deacon and lights candles reciting…)*
O Pure Light! Symbol of Divine Essence! Light of the Empyrean Realm! Make thy radiant & pure fire purge and sanctify this, thy holy altar, and my lips for the words that we are to proclaim for the greater glory of the Eternal. Amen.

As these flames lighten our way in the earthly realm, so are the great Luminaries of the Aeons ever present to illumine and enlighten our spiritual path. Come, join us now, O great Luminaries, emissaries of the Most High!

HARMOZEL
OROIAEL
DAVEITHAI
ELELETH

Come now and witness as we praise the Most High, and prepare for the celebration of the Most Holy Eucharist.

PRIEST:
Our Help is in the Lord, secret center, heart and tongue.

1st DEACON:
Whose Pure Will hath created Worlds, and fitly framed the heavens hung.

PRIEST:
Our Love is in the continuity of the Queen of Infinite Space.

2nd DEACON:
Who from Her womb hath brought all things, yet knoweth neither time nor place.

PRIEST:
Trust ye in the Pure Will.

1st DEACON:
For He gives the Mind that understandeth.

PRIEST:
Abide in the Love of Sophia forever.

2ⁿᵈ DEACON:

For that Beauty is above comparison, and the Good is inimitable, as God Himself.

PRIEST:

Blessed are the knowers of the Truth.

1ˢᵗ DEACON:

For they shall ascend to the Light.

PRIEST:

Blessed are those of the loving heart.

2ⁿᵈ DEACON:

For Love and Truth will make them free.

PRIEST:

The Truth and Love of God be with you.

CLERGY & CONGREGANTS:

And with thy spirit.

PRIEST: *(intones)*

O glorious Godhead of the Aeons, Thou, secret center, Who art surrounded by the radiant presence of the host of holy angels and messengers of Light, hear our prayers and listen to our thoughts which rise from this world of shadows, toward Thy abode of unsearchable, unspeakable, and unending Light. Amen.

Invocation of the Archangels

PRIEST:

Please rise for the Invocation of the Archangels.

ALL: *(using the forms as previously instructed)*
Ateh. Malkuth. Ve'Geburah. Ve'Gedulah. Le Olam. A-U-M

In the Name of יהוה we invoke thee, Archangel of the East, RAPHAEL!

In the Name of אדני we invoke thee, Archangel of the South, MICHAEL!

In the Name of אהיה we invoke thee, Archangel of the West, GABRIEL!

In the Name of אגלא we invoke thee, Archangel of the North, AURIEL!

Ateh. Malkuth. Ve'Geburah. Ve'Gedulah. Le Olam. A-U-M

Asperges

PRIEST: *(sprinkles blessed water while reciting…)*
Purify us, O Lord, that in Thy Power we may worthily perform the Great Work. In Thy strength, O Indwelling Lord, do we expel all forces of darkness from this, Thy Holy Altar and Sanctuary, and from this house and our own human temples wherein we worship Thee; and we pray Thee Heavenly Father, that Thou wilt command the Rulers of the Four Regions, your mighty Archangels, Lords of the Air, Water, Fire, and Earth, to build for us a Spiritual Temple through which Thy Strength

and Blessing may be poured forth upon Thy people. Through Christ our Indwelling Lord.

ALL:
So Mote It Be!

Prayer

PRIEST:
When we enter herein with all humility, let God the Almighty One enter into this Sanctuary of the Gnosis by the entrance of an eternal happiness, of a Divine prosperity, of a perfect joy, of an abundant charity, and of an eternal salutation. Let all the demons fly from this place, especially those who are opposed unto this work, and let the Angels of Peace assist and protect this Sanctuary, from which let discord and strife fly and depart. Magnify and extend upon us, O Lord, Thy most Holy Name, and bless our conversation and our assembly. Sanctify, O Lord our God, our humble entry herein, Thou the Blessed and Holy One of the Eternal Ages! Amen.

I beseech Thee, O Lord God, the All Powerful and the All Merciful, that Thou wilt deign to bless this Sanctuary, and all this place, and all those who are herein, and that Thou wilt grant unto us, who serve Thee, and rehearse nothing but the wonders of Thy Law, a good Angel for our Guardian; remove from us every adverse power; preserve us from evil and from trouble; grant, O Lord, that we may rest in this place in all safety, through Thee, O Lord, Who livest and reignest unto the Ages of the Ages.

O Lord God, All Powerful and All Merciful, Thou who desirest not the death of a sinner, but rather that he may turn from his ignorance and live; give and grant unto us Thy Grace, by ✠ Blessing and ✠ Consecrating this Altar and this Sanctuary, which is here marked out with the most powerful and holy Names of God. And may God bless this place with all the virtues of Heaven, so that no obscene or unclean spirit may have the power to enter into this Sanctuary, or to annoy any person who is therein; through our Lord Jesus, Christos, Soter, Logos, Who liveth eternally unto the Ages of the Ages. Amen.

ALL:
Amen.

Censing of the Altar

PRIEST: *(Puts incense into thurible and blesses it…)*
Creature of incense, be thou blessed in the Name of the ✠ Father, and of the ✠ Son, and of the ✠ Holy Spirit.
Priest censes the alter center, left, right.

Purify this place, O Divine and Eternal One, and make of us one mystical Body, growing into the Pleroma of your Gnosis. Make us a Spiritual Temple of living stones, through which your infinite Light may flow. Let the Holy Angels of Light join with us and assist us in this act of divine transformation. We unite now to celebrate, knowing that we all come from the Original Light, which is the Source of everything visible and invisible.

May the Lord be with you ✠

ALL:
And with thy spirit.

Confiteor

ALL:
O Lord, that which is mortal cometh not into a body immortal; but that which is immortal cometh into that which is mortal. Thou art Thou, all that is made, and all that is not made. Thou art all things, and there is nothing else Thou art not. I beseech Thee that I may never err from the Knowledge of Thee. For Thou art what I am, Thou art what I do, Thou art what I say. Amen.

PRIEST:
O Lord All Powerful, Eternal God and Father of ALL, shed upon me the Divine Influence of Thy Mercy, for I am Thy Creature. I beseech Thee to defend me from mine enemies, and to confirm in me true and steadfast faith. O Lord, I commit my Body and my Soul unto Thee, seeing I put my trust in none beside Thee; it is on Thee alone that I rely. O Lord my God aid me. O Lord hear me in the day and hour wherein I shall invoke Thee. I pray Thee by Thy Mercy not to put me into oblivion, nor to remove me from Thee. O Lord be Thou my succor, Thou Who art the God of my salvation. O Lord make me a new heart according unto Thy loving Kindness. These, O Lord, are the gifts which I await from Thee, O my God and my Master, Thou who livest and reignest unto the Ages of the Ages. Amen.

O Lord God the All Powerful One, who hast formed unto Thyself great and Ineffable Wisdom, and Co-Eternal with Thyself before the countless Ages; Thou Who before the birth of Time hast created the Aeons, and the things that they contain; Thou who hast vivified all things by Thy Holy Breath, I praise Thee, I bless Thee, I adore Thee, and I glorify Thee. Be Thou propitious unto me who am but a miserable sinner, and despise me not; save me and succor me, even me that work of Thine hands. I conjure and entreat Thee by Thy Holy Name to banish from my Spirit the darkness of Ignorance, and to enlighten me with the Fire of Thy Wisdom; take away from me all evil desires, and let not my speech be as that of the foolish. O Thou, God the Living One, whose Glory, Honor, and Kingdom shall extend unto the Ages of the Ages. Through our Lord Jesus, Christos, Soter, Logos. Amen.

DEACONS:
Amen.

Absolution

PRIEST:
God the Father ✠ God the Son ✠ God the Holy Spirit ✠ Bless ✠ Strengthen ✠ Preserve ✠ and Sanctify ✠ you. May the Lord in His loving kindness look down upon you that you may win the victory over your lower selves and receive the Grace and Comfort of the Holy Spirit.

Hear me, O Father, father of all fatherhood. I invoke you, ye forgivers of sins, ye purifiers of iniquities. Forgive the sins of the souls of these disciples, and purify their iniquities and make them worthy to be reckoned with the Kingdom of the Father of the Treasury of the Light.

Now, therefore, O Father, father of all fatherhood, let the forgivers of sins come, whose names are these:

Σιφιρψνιχευ ζενει βεριμου σοχαβριχηρ ευθαρι να ναι φιεισβαλμηριχ μευνιπος χιριε ενταιρ μουθιορ σμουρ πευχηρ οουσχους μινιονορ ισοχοβορθα.

Hear me invoking you, forgive the sins of these souls and blot out their iniquities. Let them be worthy to be reckoned with the Kingdom of the Father of the Treasury of Light.

I know the great powers and invoke them:

Αυηρ βεβρω αθρονι η ουρεφ η ωνε σουφεν κνιτουσοχρεωψ μαθωνβι μνεθωρ σουωνι χωχωετεωφ χωχε ετεωφ μεμωχ ανημφ.

Forgive the sins of these souls, blot out their iniquities which they knowingly and unknowingly have committed; forgive them then and make them worthy to be reckoned with the Kingdom of the Father, so that they are worthy to receive this Eucharistic Offering which we have come to make, Holy Father. Through our Lord Jesus, Christos, Soter, Logos. Amen.

The Lord has put away all your sins. Abide in the peace and love of the Holy Spirit.

ALL:
Amen.

Sign of Peace

PRIEST:
My Brothers and Sisters in the Gnosis, the Lord of Agape binds us with a bond of Love that cannot be broken. Therefore we invoke the indwelling Christos, Who does ever say to Thy disciples: "Peace I leave with you, My peace I give unto you." Grant us that peace and unity which are agreeable to Thy Holy Will and Commandment. In the Name of our Lord Jesus Christ, Savior and Logos, may the peace of the Lord be with you always.

CONGREGANTS:
And also with you.

Clergy & Congregants exchange Sign of Peace.

First Hermetic Discourse:
Psalm of Wisdom and Praise

PRIEST:
Which way shall I look when I praise Thee? Upward? Downward? Outward? Inward? For about Thee there is no manner, nor place, nor anything else of all things that are. But all things are in Thee; all things from Thee; Thou givest all things and takest nothing, for Thou hast all things and there is nothing that Thou hast not.

1st DEACON:

He that shall learn and study the things that are, and how they are ordered and governed, and by whom, and for what cause, or to what end, will acknowledge thanks to the Great Architect. And he that gives thanks shall be of the spirit. And he that is of the Spirit shall know both where the Truth is and what it is; and learning that, he will be yet more and more of the Spirit.

2nd DEACON:

For never shall or can that soul which, while it is in the body, lightens and lifts up itself to know and comprehend that which is Good and True, slide back to the contrary; for it is infinitely enamored thereof and forgetteth all evils; and when it hath learned and known its Father and Progenitor, it can no more apostatize or depart from that Good. That which is Good desireth to be set at liberty; but the things that are Evil love slavery.

PRIEST:

I give praise and blessing unto God the Father.

1st DEACON:

Who art everywhere the center of the sphere.

PRIEST:

I give praise and blessing unto the Mighty Mother.

2nd DEACON:

Whose circumference is nowhere found.

PRIEST:

Wisdom is to be understood in silence, and the Seed is the true Good, sown by the Will of God.

1st DEACON:

The Child of God is the Author of Regeneration. The One Man by the Will of God.

2nd DEACON:

Things of this kind are not taught, but are by God, to whom he pleaseth, brought to remembrance.

PRIEST:

I give praise and blessing unto the One.

1st DEACON:

Holy is God whose Will is performed and accomplished by his own powers.

2nd DEACON:

Holy is God that determineth to be known and is known of His, or those that are His.

PRIEST & DEACONS:

Holy art Thou, that by Thy Word hast established all things.
Holy art Thou, of Whom all Nature is the image.
Holy art Thou, Whom Nature hath not formed.
Holy art Thou, that art stronger than all power.
Holy art Thou, that art greater than all excellency.
Holy art Thou, Who art better than all praise.
O Thou unspeakable, unutterable, be praised with silence!

Pause for a moment of silent reflection.

First Reading

PRIEST:
The First Reading is taken from…

The First Lectionary Reading of the day is read by Priest.

PRIEST:
Give ear unto us, O Indwelling One, while we sing Thy praises. Thou Mystery before all uncontainables and impassables, Who did shine forth in Thy Mystery, in order that the Mystery that is from the beginning be completed in us. Hear us, O Father of boundless Light, Mother of Eternal Wisdom! All has come forth from Thee, and will return unto Thee, when the consummation of all consummations has taken place.
ALL:
Amen.

Second Hermetic Discourse:
The Secret Song

2nd DEACON:
Let all the Nature of the World entertain the hearing of this Hymn.

1ˢᵗ DEACON:

Praise ye the Lord of the Creation, and the All, and the One; the Name of the Most High be praised.

PRIEST:

Let us altogether give him blessing which rideth upon the heavens; the Creator of all Nature. This is he that is the eye of the mind, and will accept the praise of my powers.

2nd DEACON:

O all ye powers that are in me, praise the One and the All.

1ˢᵗ DEACON:

Sing together with my will, all you powers that are in me.

PRIEST:

O Holy Knowledge, being enlightened by thee I magnify the intelligible Light, and rejoice in the joy of the Lord. By me the Truth sings praise to the Truth, the Good praiseth the Good. O Life, O Light, from us unto You comes this Praise and Thanksgiving.

2ⁿᵈ DEACON:

I give thanks to Thee, the Operation of my powers.

PRIEST & DEACONS: *(with arms crossed over chest)*
A-U-M

1ˢᵗ DEACON:

I give thanks to Thee, the Power of my operations.

PRIEST & DEACONS: *(arms crossed)*
A-U-M

PRIEST:
By me Thy Word sings praise unto Thee. Receive by me this verbal sacrifice.

PRIEST & DEACONS: *(arms crossed)*
A-U-M

2nd DEACON:
The powers that are in me cry these things, they praise the All, they fulfill Thy Will; Thy Will and Counsel is from Thee unto Thee.

1st DEACON:
O All, receive a reasonable sacrifice from all things; O Life save all that is in us; O Light, enlighten, for the Mind guideth the Word.

PRIEST:
Thou art God, Thy child crieth these things unto thee, by the Fire, by the Air, by the Earth, by the Water, by the Spirit, by Thy Creatures.

PRIEST & DEACONS:
So Mote It Bel

Gnostic Canticle

PRIEST:

Faith is our Earth in which we take root.

ALL:

Amen.

PRIEST:

Hope is the Water with which we are nourished.

ALL:

Amen.

PRIEST:

Love is the Air through which we grow.

ALL:

Amen.

PRIEST:

Knowledge is the Light by which we ripen.

ALL:

Amen.

PRIEST:

It is Christ who standeth at the door of every heart. Open ye your heart unto Him that ye may be One. For as the One is in the All, so is the All in the One. Thus the Logos sayeth: As I am One with the Father, so ye are One with me. Then may ye enter that Supernal Sphere, and dwell in that great celestial mansion whose pillars are: WISDOM, STRENGTH, and BEAUTY.

Ring bell three times.

PRIEST & DEACONS: *(intone)*
Amen.

Epistle

LECTOR:
The Epistle (or Second Reading) is taken from...

The Second Lectionary Reading of the day is read by Lector.

Here endeth the Lesson.

ALL:
Thanks be to God.

Gradual

PRIEST:
He that loveth the Holy Sophia loveth Life; and they that seek her early shall be filled with Joy.

Teach me, O Lord, the way of Thy statutes, and I shall keep it unto the end. Give me understanding, and I shall keep Thy law; yea I shall keep it with my whole heart. The path of the just is as the shining light, shining more and more unto the perfect day.

Munda Cor Meum

DEACON:

Cleanse my heart and lips, O God who by the hands of Thy Seraph didst cleanse the lips of Thy prophet Isaiah with a burning coal from Thine altar, and in Thy loving kindness, so purify me that I may worthily proclaim Thy Holy Gospel. Through Christ, our Indwelling Lord. Amen.

PRIEST: *(blesses Deacon with the following words...)*
May the Lord be in thy heart and on thy lips, that through thy heart the love of God may shine forth, and through thy lips His power be made manifest. Amen.

Gospel

DEACON:

Please rise for the reading of the Gospel. The Lord be with you.

ALL:

And with thy spirit.

DEACON:

The Gospel is taken from...

As the Deacon announces the Gospel he makes the sign of the cross with the right thumb successively upon the forehead, lips, and heart.

ALL:
Glory be to Thee, O Lord.

Deacon censes the Gospel, then Gospel is read.

DEACON:
Here endeth the Gospel.

ALL:
Praise be to Thee, O Christ.

DEACON:
Be ye doers of the Word, and not hearers only.

Deacon bids people to be seated and censes the Priest, then returns to his position.

Homily and Parish announcements are given by Priest or other designated speakers.

Act of Faith

PRIEST:
Please all join me in the Act of Faith.

ALL: *(while placing right hand over heart)*
I believe in the Ineffable, Unknowable Father, incorruptible Spirit, Lord of All Worlds, Architect of all things visible and all things invisible. Light of Light.

And in the Pure Will of the Father which sends forth the Seed, which is the true Good. Life of Life.

And I believe in the Holy Spirit, Sublime Mother of the Aeons, from whose womb all things are made manifest and to which they shall return. Love of Love.

And I believe in the incarnation of our Lord Jesus Christ, self-generated and alone-begotten; creative essence of the Father; Logos of the Eternal Aeon; the Author of Regeneration, through which we may loosen the bonds of matter and recall our own divine nature, and become one in the fullness of God. Liberty of Liberty.

And I believe in the communion of the Holy Saints and Prophets.

And I believe in the miracle of the Eucharist, whereby the elements of Bread and Wine are transmuted into the Body and Blood of Christ the Logos, giving us Spiritual sustenance, and a visible means of grace.

And I believe in One Universal and Apostolic Church of Light, Life, Love, and Liberty.

A-U-M A-U-M A-U-M

Invocation of the Holy Guardian Angel

PRIEST:

O You, divine Spirit! Spirit of Wisdom, Strength, and Beauty; powerful Being of Light, with whom I desire to accomplish the most intimate union!

I call you! I invoke you! Come to my assistance; guide my steps on the Path of Regeneration during this whole day. Vivify me with that Divine Love that enflames you; send me continually your intellect; give me the weapons that I need in order to vanquish my spiritual enemies.

Guide my steps toward the Truth; I abandon myself to your direction with total confidence.

Divine Logos, that have deigned to send Your Angels to guard and guide us, help me profit from their powerful operations; help me be preserved from any fall during this day.

Let me come to know intimately this Spirit, to which you have particularly entrusted me.

I ask this Grace by Your Holy Blood, that has become the sigil of my reconciliation with you. Amen.

Offertorium

PRIEST: *(removes veil, pall, etc.)*
Come Thou Holy Name of Christ, Name above all names;
come power from above and come highest gift; Thou Knower
of the Chosen's Mysteries descend; Thou Who dost share in all
noble strivers' struggles; Come! Come Thou Who givest joy to
all who are at one with Thee; come and commune with us in
this Eucharist which we are about to make in Thy Name, in
this Sacrament to which we have assembled at Thy call.

Αεηιουω ιαω αωι ωια ψινωθερ θερνωψ νωψιθερ ζαγουρη
παγουρη νεθμομαωθ νεψιομωθ μαραχαχθα θωβαρραβαυ
θαρναχαχαν ζοροκοθορα ιεου Σαβαωθ.

Priest elevates paten with both hands.

Blessed are You, O God, who art the Source of all things
visible and invisible; the Lord of Light, Life, Love, and Liberty.
We offer this bread, grain of the Earth, transformed by human
hands, as a token of our terrestrial nature. May it transform us
and be the BODY OF CHRIST.

ALL:
Blessed be God forever.

*Priest returns paten. Acolyte pours wine and a little water into the
Chalice.*

PRIEST:
Remembering the psychic and pneumatic natures of the Master
Jesus, and our own psychic and pneumatic natures, we mix

water with this wine, praying that we may abide in His Consciousness and He in us.

Priest elevates Chalice with both hands.

Blessed are you O God who art the source of all things visible and invisible, the Lord of Light, Life, Love, and Liberty. We offer this wine, fruit of the Earth, transformed by human hands, as a token of our celestial nature. May it transform us and be the BLOOD OF CHRIST.

ALL:
Blessed be God forever.

Second Censing

PRIEST: *(places more incense on charcoal)*
Be thou blessed in the Name of the ✠ Father, and of the ✠ Son, and of the ✠ Holy Spirit.

God the Father, seen of none, God the Co-Eternal Son, and God the Holy Spirit who givest us life, pour forth Thy threefold power into these our oblations.

As this incense rises before Thee, O Lord, so let our prayer ascend Thy Holy Realms.

Glory be to the Unknown Father ✠ to the Son the Divine Logos ✠ and to the Holy Spirit ✠ our Celestial Mother and Consoler.

Lavabo

PRIEST: *(washes hands)*
O Heavenly Father, as Your rains cleanse and purify the earth, I wash my hands so that they too may be cleansed of the impurities of this world.

Asperges me hyssopo - et mundabor. Lavabis me aqua et super nivem dealbabor!

Orate Fratres

PRIEST:
My Brothers and Sisters, we have built a temple for the distribution of the power of the Logos. Let us prepare these gifts as a channel for its reception. Receive, O Source of all things visible and invisible, this Sacrifice of bread and wine. And may our lives be forever sanctified in Your service by the power of Christ, our Indwelling Lord. Amen.

Prayer Over the Gifts

PRIEST:
May we who partake of this Holy sacrament receive the power of Your Light and Life and be forever joined in Your Holy Wisdom.

ALL:
Amen.

Prayer to the Holy Spirit

PRIEST:
O Holy Spirit, Barbelo, Divine Mother of All, may you receive us with your Glorious Embrace. Thou Who hast made Thyself known to us through your emissaries of Light and Life, of Love and Liberty; Your Aeon Sophia and her daughter Zoe, whose heavenly archetypes have been mirrored here on earth in the persons of Eve, Norea, the Virgin Mary, and Mary Magdalene; and known in the celestial realm as the Woman Clothed with the Sun; may You open our ears that we may hear Your voice of Understanding, and open our hearts that we may pour forth Thy Love.

Eucharistic Prayer

PRIEST:
O Most High God, You are holy indeed, and all creation rightly gives You praise. All life, all holiness comes from You through Christ, our Lord, Logos of the Eternal Aeon. From age to age, You reveal Your perennial Wisdom to Your Holy Elect, and call forth those that might partake of Your Divine Mystery.

Joins hands, holding them outstretched over the offerings.

Epiclesis

And so, Most High God, we bring You these gifts. We ask You to make them holy by Your power to bless ✠ to approve ✠ and to ratify ✠ that they may become the Body ✠ and Blood ✠ of Christ, the Logos.

Raises bread slightly.

Institution

Following the example set forth by Melchizedek, the eternal High Priest, the Master Jesus, took bread and gave You thanks and praise. He blessed and broke the bread and gave it to His disciples, and said:

Bows slightly.

Take and eat ye all of this, for **THIS IS MY BODY**.

Shows consecrated host to the people, places on paten and genuflects in adoration.

In like manner, when the supper was ended, he took the noble Chalice.

Raises Chalice a little.

Again he gave You thanks and praise, blessed it and gave it to His disciples, and said:

Bows slightly.

Take and drink ye all of this, for **THIS IS MY BLOOD**. Do this in remembrance of me.

Shows Chalice; returns Chalice and genuflects in adoration.

Extends hands.

Father, we celebrate the memory of Christ, the Eternal Logos, the repairer and our restorer of Gnosis. We, Your people and Your Priests offer unto You, O Most High God, this perfect sacrifice: the bread of Life and the cup of eternal Salvation.

Look with favor on these offerings and accept them as once You accepted the gifts of our patriarch in the Gnosis, the bread and wine offered by Your priest Melchizedek.

Almighty God, we pray that this sacrifice be borne to thine altar, there to be offered by Him who, as the eternal High Priest, forever offers Himself as the eternal sacrifice.
And as He has ordained that the heavenly sacrifice shall be mirrored here on earth through the ministry of mortals, to the end that Your holy people may be brought more closely into fellowship with You, we do pray for them who serve at this altar, that rightly celebrating the mysteries of the Most Holy Body ✠ and Blood ✠ of the Christ, they may be filled ✠ with Your mighty power and blessing, O Lord of Light, Life, Love, and Liberty.

Litany

The Litany may be shortened or lengthened as required.

PRIEST:

Let us now in due and ancient fashion call upon the powers of the Most High and on all the Holy Ones who were and are and are to come, that united with them we may bravely strive for and ultimately attain to the Gnosis of Light, Life, Love, and Liberty.

All face West and kneel

PRIEST:
I-A-O

DEACONS:
Shed thy glory upon us.

PRIEST:
Sabaoth

DEACONS:
Shed thy glory upon us.

PRIEST:
Abraxas

DEACONS:
Shed thy glory upon us.

PRIEST:
Sophia

DEACONS:
Shed thy glory upon us.

PRIEST:
All the souls of the Holy Gnostics during the Aeons.

DEACONS:
Hear us and be near us.

PRIEST:
Holy Mary Magdalene

DEACONS:
Hear us and be near us.

PRIEST:
Holy John the Baptist

DEACONS:
Hear us and be near us.

PRIEST:
Holy John the Evangelist

DEACONS:
Hear us and be near us.

PRIEST:
Holy Thomas

DEACONS:
Hear us and be near us.

PRIEST:
Holy Philip

DEACONS:
Hear us and be near us.

PRIEST:
Holy Simon Magus

DEACONS:
Hear us and be near us.

PRIEST:
Holy Dositheus

DEACONS:
Hear us and be near us.

PRIEST:
Holy Menander

DEACONS:
Hear us and be near us.

PRIEST:
Holy Saturninus

DEACONS:
Hear us and be near us.

PRIEST:
Holy Basilides

DEACONS:
Hear us and be near us.

PRIEST:
Holy Valentinus

DEACONS:
Hear us and be near us.

PRIEST:
Holy Bardaisan

DEACONS:
Hear us and be near us.

PRIEST:
Holy Clement of Alexandria

DEACONS:
Hear us and be near us.

PRIEST:
Holy Origen

DEACONS:
Hear us and be near us.

PRIEST:
Holy Hypatia

DEACONS:
Hear us and be near us.

PRIEST:
Holy Esclaremonde & all Cathar Martyrs

DEACONS:
Hear us and be near us.

PRIEST:
Holy Joachim

DEACONS:
Hear us and be near us.

PRIEST:
Holy Jacque de Molay & all the Blessed Templars

DEACONS:
Hear us and be near us.

PRIEST:
Holy Martinez de Pasqually

DEACONS:
Hear us and be near us.

PRIEST:
Holy Louis Claude de Saint-Martin

DEACONS:
Hear us and be near us.

PRIEST:
Holy Jean-Baptiste Willermoz

DEACONS:
Hear us and be near us.

PRIEST:
Holy Bernard-Raymond Fabré-Palaprat

DEACONS:
Hear us and be near us.

PRIEST:
Holy Lady Caithness

DEACONS:
Hear us and be near us.

PRIEST:
Holy Tau Valentin II

DEACONS:
Hear us and be near us.

PRIEST:
Holy Mar Timotheus I

DEACONS:

Hear us and be near us.

PRIEST:

Holy Jean Sempé

DEACONS:

Hear us and be near us.

PRIEST:

Holy Abbé Julio

DEACONS:

Hear us and be near us.

PRIEST:

Holy Tau Vincent

DEACONS:

Hear us and be near us.

PRIEST:

Holy Jean II

DEACONS:

Hear us and be near us.

PRIEST:

Holy Tau Harmonious

DEACONS:

Hear us and be near us.

PRIEST:
Holy Tau Jean III

DEACONS:
Hear us and be near us.

PRIEST:
Holy Tau Ogdoade Orfeo I

DEACONS:
Hear us and be near us.

PRIEST:
Holy Tau Ogdoade Orfeo III

DEACONS:
Hear us and be near us.

PRIEST:
Holy Tau Johannes XIII

DEACONS:
Hear us and be near us.

PRIEST:
Holy Tau Iohannes Harmonius

DEACONS:
Hear us and be near us.

PRIEST:
All the Apostles, Prophets, Bishops, Priests, & Martyrs of the Gnosis.

DEACONS:
Hear us and be near us, now and forever.

Kyrie

PRIEST:
Kyrie Eleison

ALL:
Kyrie Eleison

PRIEST:
Christe Eleison

ALL:
Christe Eleison

PRIEST & ALL:
Kyrie Eleison

PRIEST:
Welcome into Your kingdom, O Lord, our departed brothers and sisters in the Gnosis.

Mother and Father united as one;
Wisdom and Strength through Your eternal Son;
We are divided for Love's sake;

That through our union we may make Ourselves as symbols of Heaven on Earth; In life, in death, and in rebirth!

O Christ our Lord who gives us all these gifts, bless them and make them holy.

Pater Noster

PRIEST:

Let us pray with confidence to the Father in the words the Master Jesus gave us.

ALL:

Our Father who art in Heaven, hallowed by Thy Name; Thy kingdom come, Thy will be done,

On Earth as it is in Heaven. Give us this day, our daily bread, And forgive us our debts, as we have also forgiven our debtors.

And leave us not in temptation, but deliver us from evil,

For Thine is the Kingdom, and the Power, and the Glory, forever and ever. Amen.

PRIEST: *(with hands extended)*

Deliver us Lord from the evil of ignorance, and grant us peace, love, and light in our day.

Breaking of the Bread

PRIEST:

O Divine Light, You show Yourself this day upon countless altars and yet are one and indivisible. In token of Thy great Sacrifice, we rend *(break bread)* this, Thy Holy Body, that we may be as Thou art.

Through this ancient and sacred tradition, all Heaven and Earth are united in Thy Consciousness, Thy Love, and Thy Will. And as the One became many, only to restore all to the Pleroma, so too, in the breaking of this bread, we are one with Thee, as Thou art one with the Father.

> *Breaks off small piece of bread from the left half, makes sign of the cross over the Chalice, and places piece in Chalice; then blows three crosses of air over Chalice.*
> *Intones…*

Through Him, and with Him, and in Him;
In the Unity of the Holy Spirit;
All glory and honor are Yours Almighty Father,
Forever and ever.

ALL: *(intone)*
Amen.

PRIEST:

Let us pray. Adoration be to Thee, O Most High God, Father of all Fatherhood, and to Thee, O Mother of all, who in the incarnation of Your Logos have mystically provided us with the Sacrament of His Body and Blood, that by partaking of this

Mystery, we may reunite within ourselves the fragments of Your Divinity dispersed throughout the Cosmos. Holy, Holy, Holy, are You, the Father and Mother of the Treasury of the Light, now and unto the countless ages. Amen.

Theurgic Consecration

Priest takes Dagger, faces East, and draws the letter YOD in the air with Dagger as it is pronounced, then intones the Holy Name, thus:

By the virtue of ׳ I call forth the power of IAO to join in this Holy Sacrifice.

Priest travels to the South via the North and West, that is, by walking 270° counterclockwise, draws the letter HE, and intones the Holy Name, thus:

By the virtue of ה I call forth the power of SABAOTH to join in this Holy Sacrifice.

Priest continues 210° counterclockwise to the West, draws the letter VAV, and intones the Holy Name, thus:

By the virue of ו I call forth the power of ABRAXAS to join in this Holy Sacrifice.

Priest continues 270° to the North, draws the letter HE, and intones the Holy Name, thus:

By the virtue of **ה** I call forth the power of SOPHIA to join in this Holy Sacrifice.

Priest travels 210° counterclockwise again to return to the East for the third complete circuit. He faces the Eucharistic Altar, and with arms outstretched and holding the Dagger in the right hand...

The Son would not be the Father without wearing the Father's Name. So by the Power of the Holy Tetragrammaton, and by the virtue of the Tri-Unity of the Holy Letter **ש** *(draws Hebrew letter with Dagger in the air above Chalice)*, I call forth the power of the Author of Regeneration, the Repairer of Souls, the Destroyer of Death...

Intones while slowly lowering Dagger with both hands into Chalice.

יהשוה to pour forth Thy powers into this Holy Sacrifice and transmute these elements of bread and wine into the Divine Body and Blood of the Logos.

Makes three crosses in Chalice with Dagger.

Communion

PRIEST: *(Elevating the Body and Blood)*
Behold the Divine Light which lighteth every man that cometh into the world. May the communion of these Holy Mysteries be to the regeneration of both soul and body. Let us draw nigh and receive this most Holy Sacrament.

Ablutions and silent meditation.

Post Eucharistic Prayer

ALL:

May we, who in this Holy Mystery have entered into the all-pervading strength and love of Christ our Indwelling Lord, be guided by the Divine Presence into the fullness of Truth, that we may attain to that mount of vision whereon we may see the boundless light unveiled in the wholeness of its Divine Glory. Amen.

Third Hermetic Discourse: Concluding Rite

PRIEST:

If thou wilt not equal thyself to God, thou canst not understand God. Increase thyself unto an immeasurable greatness, leaping beyond every body and transcending all time; become eternity and thou shalt understand God. If thou believe in thyself that nothing is impossible, but accountest thyself immortal, thou canst understand all things; every art, every science, and the manner and custom of every living thing.

1st DEACON:

Become higher than all height, lower than all depths, comprehend in thyself the qualities of all the Creatures of the Fire, the Water, the Dry and Moist; and conceive likewise, that thou canst at once be everywhere in the Sea, in the Earth, in the Air.

2nd DEACON:

Thou shalt at once understand thyself, not yet begotten, in the womb, young, old, to be dead, the things after death, and all these together; as also times, places, deeds, qualities, quantities; or else thou canst not yet understand God.

PRIEST & DEACONS:

For the Light is One and its Mystery is a hiddenness beyond our senses and beyond the vision of our eyes.

PRIEST:

In all things that are, are the senses, because they cannot be without them.

1st DEACON:

But Gnosis differs much from sense; for sense is of the things that surmount it, but Gnosis is the end of sense.

2nd DEACON:

Gnosis is the gift of God; for all Gnosis is unbodily, but useth the Mind as an instrument, as the Mind uses the body.

PRIEST & DEACONS:

Therefore I believe Thee, and bear witness and go into the Life and Light.

PRIEST:

The Life and Light of God be with you.

ALL:
And with thy spirit.

Dismissal

PRIEST:
From our sanctuary here, may the Light be spread throughout the world. May Christ the Logos of the Eternal Aeon, show you the Light that you seek, give you His comfort and compassion, and lead you to true Wisdom.

Solomon in his great wisdom said to his son: Do thou, O my son Roboam, remember, that the fear of the Lord is only the beginning of Wisdom. Keep and preserve those who have not Understanding in the Fear of the Lord, which will give and will preserve unto thee my crown. But learn to triumph thyself over Fear by Wisdom, and the Spirits will descend from Heaven to serve thee.

I, Solomon, thy father, King of Israel and Palmyra, I have sought out and obtained in my lot the Holy Chokmah, which is the Wisdom of Adonai. And I have become King of the Spirits, as well of Heaven as of Earth, Master of the Dwellers of the Air, and of the Living Souls of the Sea, because I was in possession of the Key of the Hidden Gates of Light.

There is a peace that passes all understanding; it abides in the hearts of those who live in the eternal now. There is a power that makes all things new; it lives and moves in those who know themselves as one.

May that peace abide with you; may that power lift you up to the awareness wherein dwells the Christ, so that you may look with your eyes unveiled upon His most Holy Countenance and there see your true self revealed.

And may the blessing of the Mystery of the Three-in-One, of God the Unknown Father ✠ of Christ the redeeming and ever-coming Logos ✠ and of the Holy Spirit our celestial Mother and Consoler ✠ descend upon you and remain with you always. Amen.

Ite, missa est.

ALL:
Deo gratias.

www.ingramcontent.com/pod-product-compliance
Lightning Source LLC
Chambersburg PA
CBHW071738020426
42331CB00008B/2079